BATWOMAN
elegy

BATWOMAN
elegy

GREG RUCKA WRITER

J.H WILLIAMS III ARTIST

DAVE STEWART COLORIST

TODD KLEIN LETTERS

BATMAN CREATED BY **BOB KANE**

MICHAEL SIGLAIN EDITOR-ORIGINAL SERIES
HARVEY RICHARDS ASSISTANT EDITOR-ORIGINAL SERIES
IAN SATTLER DIRECTOR EDITORIAL, SPECIAL PROJECTS
AND ARCHIVAL EDITIONS
ANTON KAWASAKI EDITOR
ROBBIN BROSTERMAN DESIGN DIRECTOR-BOOKS
EDDIE BERGANZA EXECUTIVE EDITOR
BOB HARRAS VP – EDITOR IN CHIEF

DC COMICS
DIANE NELSON PRESIDENT
DAN DIDIO AND **JIM LEE** CO-PUBLISHERS
GEOFF JOHNS CHIEF CREATIVE OFFICER
JOHN ROOD EVP – SALES, MARKETING AND BUSINESS DEVELOPMENT
AMY GENKINS SENIOR VP – BUSINESS AND LEGAL AFFAIRS
NAIRI GARDINER SENIOR VP – FINANCE
JEFF BOISON VP – PUBLISHING OPERATIONS
MARK CHIARELLO VP – ART DIRECTION AND DESIGN
JOHN CUNNINGHAM VP – MARKETING
TERRI CUNNINGHAM VP – TALENT RELATIONS AND SERVICES
ALISON GILL SENIOR VP – MANUFACTURING AND OPERATIONS
DAVID HYDE VP – PUBLICITY
HANK KANALZ SENIOR VP – DIGITAL
JAY KOGAN VP – BUSINESS AND LEGAL AFFAIRS, PUBLISHING
JACK MAHAN VP – BUSINESS AFFAIRS, TALENT
NICK NAPOLITANO VP – MANUFACTURING ADMINISTRATION
RON PERAZZA VP – ONLINE
SUE POHJA VP – BOOK SALES
COURTNEY SIMMONS SENIOR VP – PUBLICITY
BOB WAYNE SENIOR VP – SALES

Cover by J.H. Williams III
Publication design by Robbie Biederman

BATWOMAN: ELEGY

Published by DC Comics. Cover, introduction and compilation
Copyright © 2010 DC Comics. All Rights Reserved.

Originally published in single magazine form in DETECTIVE COMICS
#854-860. Copyright © 2009, 2010 DC Comics. All Rights Reserved.
All characters, their distinctive likenesses and related elements
featured in this publication are trademarks of DC Comics.
The stories, characters and incidents featured in this
publication are entirely fictional. DC Comics does not
read or accept unsolicited submissions of ideas, stories
or artwork.

DC Comics, 1700 Broadway, New York, NY 10019
A Warner Bros. Entertainment Company
Printed by Quad/Graphics, Dubuque, IA, USA. 5/06/11.
First Printing. ISBN: 978-1-4012-3146-0

Introduction

BY RACHEL **MADDOW**

I confess to once giving a copy of Greg Rucka's *Queen and Country: Operation Broken Ground* to a member of the Senate Intelligence Committee, because I thought it might be helpful to the Senator. It's not as crazy as it sounds: get to know Rucka's character Tara Chase and then Google the real modern American spook Dusty Foggo, and see which one you find more edifying.

In Batwoman, Katherine Rebecca Kane is another character written by Rucka that you can't quite believe doesn't exist in the real world. Her recitation of West Point's honor code — "A cadet shall not lie, cheat or steal, nor suffer others to do so" — rings in my ears like Lieutenant Dan Choi reciting the same code to me on television in March 2009, proving that the "Don't Ask, Don't Tell" policy forced him to lie as a condition of his military service.

In Kate Kane's quiet but life-defining drive to serve, there's the veterans of my generation who in the absence of a draft but through nine straight years of war, have done three, four, five combat tours, to come home to a nation that doesn't always quite remember we're at war.

"When you act wrongly, you have to answer for it. Without hiding, without complaint.... That's integrity, and it is the foundation of honor." That's the moral spine on which Kate Kane's battered frame is hung. She is brave and surly and hurt and strong and always on the Batman rule. For all the brilliant literary allusion, mystery, and trademark Rucka attention to detail, what you won't be able to shake when you're done here is that damn compelling lead character.

Well, maybe that and the art.

In a single, wordless panel showing Kate's father's reaction after she tells him why she's been separated from the Army, artist J.H. Williams III captures both a turning point between characters, and a nation's point of decision. It actually feels, right now, in America, the way Colonel Kane looks in that panel, hurt by the plain open ask of his daughter's green eyes.

Yes, cyanogen chloride is a real thing. No, "Southern Misunderstandistan" is not a real place, but you can bet I'll steal it for commenting on our wars, if I haven't done so already by the time you read this. Yes, some of the baddies in the true religion of crime are super genderqueer and yes, guns mix with magic. Get over it. It's all true, it's all gutwrenching, and you love it.

I won't lie to you: I would read anything Greg Rucka wrote. I would read Greg Rucka's grocery lists. I would read Greg Rucka's discarded edits. I would read a Greg Rucka forty-volume soft-hearted navel-gazer about characters I couldn't care less about, if he was capable of writing such a thing, and if he did I'd probably read it out loud to my friends and exclaim and swear about how he made me care.

Batwoman's in good hands here. You'll see.

Rachel Maddow
March, 2010

Rachel Maddow is a political commentator and television host. She has been the anchorwoman of several syndicated talk radio programs and is currently the host of the nightly television program The Rachel Maddow Show on MSNBC.

There was a year, not so very long past, where the world turned without the eyes of its three greatest heroes looking upon it, when Batman, Superman, and Wonder Woman stepped back from their roles.

It was in Gotham City, then, that the symbol of the red bat was first truly noted, though some have speculated that both it and its wearer had been there for quite some time already, watching and waiting. But it was not until the Dark Knight's absence that this new presence became truly known.

This new hero was, in many ways, a reflection of the Batman — the same ruthless pursuit of justice; the same savage need to defend the innocent. But this was not some Robin all-grown-up, nor was it some boy raised to fit boots he had no hope of being able to fill.

This was a woman, the Batwoman, and while there was, indeed, a reflection, it was clear to all who saw her that this was something different. This was not another devotee of the Dark Knight. This woman went her own way.

At the end of this year, the Batwoman fell, captured by a cult devoted to evil, a cult that saw in her the fulfillment of its dark destiny. It was the hand of the cult's leader, the High Madame of the Religion of Crime, that drove a knife into the heart of Batwoman.

She should have died. She nearly did. Instead, it was the High Madame who fell, and the Batwoman who survived. But a wound to the heart is not one easily healed.

It has been a long road back, and now the Batwoman hears whispers in the night: a new High Madame is coming to Gotham.

The Batwoman is looking forward to meeting her....

ONE AGITATO

TODD KLEIN: letters

TODD KLEIN
letters

End of
ELEGY

TWENTY YEARS AGO

GREG RUCKA
WRITER
DAVE STEWART
COLORS

J.H. WILLIAMS III
ARTIST
TODD KLEIN
LETTERS

SEVEN YEARS AGO

GREG RUCKA
WRITER
DAVE STEWART
COLORS

J.H. WILLIAMS III
ARTIST
TODD KLEIN
LETTERS

SPECIAL THANKS TO 1LT DANIEL CHOI (USMA 2003) FOR HIS GENEROUS ASSISTANCE IN RESEARCH FOR THIS ISSUE

FOUR YEARS AGO

"MAKE NO MISTAKE: YOU DO THIS, YOU'RE GOING TO *WAR*.

"DEFINE THE *GOAL*. DEFINE THE *OBJECTIVE*. DEFINE THE *TERMS* OF *VICTORY*.

"BECAUSE IF VICTORY MEANS BRINGING YOUR MOTHER AND SISTER BACK, YOU'VE *ALREADY* LOST.

"...TO KEEP *ONE* PERSON FROM HAVING THEIR LIFE *SHATTERED* IN VIOLENCE...

"...AND TO COME HOME *ALIVE* WHEN YOU'RE DONE...

"IF VICTORY MEANS TAKING *REVENGE* FOR WHAT HAPPENED TO THEM, YOU'VE *ALREADY* LOST.

"BUT IF THE OBJECTIVE IS TO SAVE JUST *ONE* LIFE...

"...TO PROTECT *ONE* INNOCENT...

"...THEN YOU CAN *PREVAIL.*

"AND GOD HELP WHATEVER POOR BASTARD TRIES TO *STAND* IN YOUR *WAY.*"

Detective Comics
VARIANT COVER GALLERY

Bonus Material
BY J.H. WILLIAMS III & GREG RUCKA

BATWOMAN - CHARACTER SHEET - ROUGHS

THESE CHANGES TO CURRENT COSTUME KEEP THE SAME BASIC LOOK BUT ADD
MORE SENSIBILITY AND FUNCTIONALITY

HAIR WILL BE A DETACHABLE WIG

CAPE FASTENS IN THE
FRONT TO LOWER SHOULDER-
UPPER CHEST AREA

MORE
HEAVY ARMORED
ARM BRACERS THAT
ARE SEPARATE
FROM GLOVES -
GLOVES TUCK
UNDER BRACER AT
WRIST -

BELT IS FASTENED
AND NO LONGER
LOOSE - FITS
TIGHTLY

CAPE IS MUCH
LONGER - DRACULA-
ESQUE

NOTE - THE CAPE
ONLY COMES TO
FIVE POINTS
FORMING A VERY
CLEARLY STYLIZED
GIANT RED BAT
DESIGN WHEN
COMPLETELY
UNFURLED

BOOTS ARE NOW
MORE REALISTIC
TO PURPOSE - NOTE
ON ADDITIONAL
DRAWING THEY ZIP
UP ON THE SIDE

KATHY KANE · CHARACTER SHEET · ROUGHS
A COMPLETELY DIFFERENT LOOK THAN PREVIOUSLY
MORE DEFINITIVE PERSONALITY — RETRO-ROCKABILLY LOOK
SHE IS REALLY INTO ALTERNATIVE AND EDGY MUSIC —
   A BIT OF PUNK — PSYCHOBILLY — GOTH AND REFLECTS THIS IN HER
   PERSONAL STYLE — THIS LOOK HERE IS JUST ONE ASPECT

HER SKIN IS LITERALLY
VAMPIRE WHITE PORCELAIN
VERY LITTLE COLOR AT
   ALL

BLUE BIRD
TATTOO

EYES ARE GREEN
AND SHE WEARS DARK
   RED LIPSTICK
COOL TONED EYE
SHADOW

LARGE
NAUTICAL STAR
TATTOO

WHITE BOW

These two pages reveal the original script by Greg Rucka for DETECTIVE COMICS #857, pages 18 & 19 – followed by the original black and white art for the pages by J.H. Williams III, without coloring or lettering.

Jim – This is the mirror spread.

ONE:
Full body shot, BATWOMAN. Iconic. More an art element, as discussed, than an actual storytelling panel. This is the mirror to Panel Eight.

NO COPY.

TWO:
Interior of the MAIN COMPARTMENT, as BATWOMAN enters.

ALICE is standing at the PUMP CONTROLS, and she's livid. The fucking thing's broken! This isn't fair! Nothing's fair!! Maybe she's holding one of the BROKEN WHEELS in one hand.

In her OTHER HAND, she's holding a PISTOL, pointed at BATWOMAN.

1 BATWOMAN:	You're done, High Madame.
2 BATWOMAN:	I **disabled** the pump, you're not killing **anyone** today.
3 ALICE:	I ca'n't **stand** this any **longer!**

THREE:
BATWOMAN shielding herself with her CAPE – covering her head with it – as ALICE empties the GUN at her. The BARRAGE of shots is knocking BATWOMAN to a knee.

ALICE is screaming at BATWOMAN as she fires.

4 ALICE:	And as for you!
5 ALICE:	As for you, I'll shake you into a kitten, that I will!!!

6 SFX:	BLAMMBLAMMBLAMMBLAMMBLAMMBLAMMklk klkklk

FOUR:
BATWOMAN, on one knee, lowering the CAPE to look.

ALICE has dropped the gun, already going out the ROOF HATCH. Maybe just her legs visible as she climbs out.

7 BATWOMAN:	Dammit, **stop!**

[continued]

FIVE:
Exterior of the plane, ALICE is pulling herself along the wing on hands and knees to reach one of the CANISTERS, determined to succeed. The WIND whips her hair and clothes violently.

BATWOMAN is just emerging from the HATCH behind her, shouting at her. Her GRAPPLING GUN is in her hand.

8 BATWOMAN: It's **over**, Alice!

SIX:
BATWOMAN fires the GRAPPLING GUN, the line catching ALICE around one ANKLE.

ALICE has grabbed the CANNISTER RIG with one hand, holding on to it, and with the other is pointing her REMAINING PISTOL back at BATWOMAN.

She's crying uncontrollably. She doesn't want to lose. She can't lose. If she loses, who is she?

9 SFX: paff

10 ALICE: The **face** is what one **goes** by, generally.

SEVEN:
ALICE SHOOTS, hitting the GRAPPLING GUN in BATWOMAN'S HAND

BATWOMAN is losing the GRAPPLING GUN, obviously.

11 SFX: BLAMMM

12 BATWOMAN: ahg!

13 ALICE: Who am **I**, then?

EIGHT:
Full body shot, ALICE, iconic, the mirror image of Panel One.

NO COPY.

These two pages reveal the original script by Greg Rucka for DETECTIVE COMICS #859,
pages 8 & 9 – followed by the original black and white art for the pages by
J.H. Williams III, without coloring or lettering.

ONE:
Wash in on the SYMBOL of the Kane Heresy, the Dark Faith's circle emblem, with a CHALICE on its side, spilling WINE or BLOOD.

We *may* be able to see the top of ABBOT'S HEAD in this panel.

For the record, the Heresy is based in the ruins of pre-No Man's Land Gotham, in what was once a small church before the earthquake. The location serves as a combination place of worship, as well as a dormitory/home for those members of the Heresy unable to control their change, ie, those Monster Men who can't, for whatever reason, revert their forms to "human."

They try to keep it nice, here, but let's face it – it's an old church that was damaged in an earthquake and is buried under ground. How nice can that be? Thing to remember is that Alice's Dark Faith has bucks; Abbot's has nada.

1 ABBOT:	My story. Listen, because it is yours, too.
2 ABBOVE:	The prophesy is told in The Blasphemies, in the Book of Lilith.
3 ABBOT:	That on the eighteenth day past the feast of All Saints…

TWO:
Angle, past Doctor MALLORY KIMBALL, as she enters her office at St. Luke's Hospital, in Gotham.

MALLORY has stopped short, reacting to BATWOMAN standing in her office.

Jim, I'd like to play this differently than in a Batman title, if that makes sense – in a Batman book, Mallory would enter the office, and then we'd see Batman come out of the shadows behind her or something like that. I don't want to do that here with Kate; it's against her character, and frankly we've seen it a million times before.

With that in mind, yes, Batwoman has been waiting for Mallory, but she's not trying to scare her or ninja-tactics her. Not sure where this should put her in the room, or what pose she should be in, but she's been waiting.

BATWOMAN still has the injuries she was carrying last issue – the conceit is that all of the "present" stuff is taking place the same night, which is also the same night as the events of issues 3 and 4.

This means BATWOMAN may still be bleeding from one or two of her various wounds – that stab wound that Alice gave her in the arm is particularly nasty.

4 BATWOMAN:	Doctor Kimball.
5 BATWOMAN:	I need a **favor**.

THREE:
Back to ABBOT, panning down a bit, maybe swinging around to look at him, as if he's speaking directly to us. He's wearing his human form.

6 ABBOT:	…the Apostle of the First would come to Gotham…
7 ABBOT:	…and there he would murder the "Twice-Named Daughter of Cain."

FOUR:
BATWOMAN is holding out the TWO SAMPLE TUBES from last issue, offering them to MAL-
LORY. BATWOMAN is doing this with her wounded arm.

MALLORY is reacting to the sight of the STAB WOUND on Batwoman.

8 BATWOMAN:	I need a DNA test run on these samples.
9 BATWOMAN:	I need to confirm they're from **monozygotic** twins.

10 MALLORY:	You're **wounded**.
11 BATWOMAN:	Will you do this for me?

FIVE:
On ABBOT. He's beginning to transform into his WOLFMAN form.

12 ABBOT:	So many times, the High Madame poured these words in my ear.
13 ABBOT:	So many times, it had to be the **truth**.

SIX:
MALLORY has taken the samples in one hand, already setting them aside. With her other hand, she's
taken BATWOMAN'S wounded arm by the WRIST. Mallory is clearly concerned about the wound.

BATWOMAN is still in the same place she was last issue, and she's barely feeling the injury, now.
Focused entirely on Mallory – the injury doesn't matter, what matters is the DNA test, that's the only
thing she cares about right now.

14 MALLORY:	You've been **stabbed**—
15 BATWOMAN:	Doctor Kimball. Mallory. Will you test them for me?
16 MALLORY:	I can have the results by tomorrow night. Now take off your gauntlet, let me take a look at—

SEVEN:
On ABBOT, and he's fully transformed now. Growling out his words.

17 ABBOT:	It rrrr had to be grrr **truth**.

EIGHT:
MALLORY reacting.

BATWOMAN has pulled her hand back, already turning, heading to the window. Business here is
done, time to go.

18 BATWOMAN:	I'll be back tomorrow night.

NINE:
Tight on ABBOT, his WEREWOLF EYES.

19 ABBOT:	It rrrr **wasn't**.

GREG **RUCKA**

is a thriller novelist who became one of the premier writers for
DC Comics in the last decade. His work on BATMAN brought fresh attention
to the character and the inhabitants of Gotham City. Additionally, he won the
Eisner award for best story with GOTHAM CENTRAL's "Half a Life." His other DC credits
include ADVENTURES OF SUPERMAN, CHECKMATE, DETECTIVE COMICS, WONDER WOMAN,
ACTION COMICS and 52. Rucka is married to fellow writer Jen Van Meter and they make
their home in Portland, Oregon.

J.H. **WILLIAMS III**

entered the comics field in 1991 and immediately began getting attention for his finely crafted
work on such titles as BATMAN, STARMAN and his co-creation (with D. Curtis Johnson), CHASE.
His acclaimed artistry was later seen on SON OF SUPERMAN, SEVEN SOLIDERS OF VICTORY and
JONAH HEX, and he has received multiple Eisner nominations for his work on co-creations
DESOLATION JONES (with Warren Ellis), and PROMETHEA (with Alan Moore).
Williams and his wife, Wendy, live in California.

DAVE **STEWART**

began his career as an intern at Dark Horse Comics, and then quickly moved into
coloring comics. His impressive credits include DC: THE NEW FRONTIER, HUMAN TARGET,
SUPERMAN/BATMAN, CATWOMAN: WHEN IN ROME, *Captain America*, *Daredevil*,
Joss Whedon's *Fray*, Mike Mignola's *Hellboy: The Third Wish* and *B.P.R.D.*, Gerard Way's
The Umbrella Academy, and Michael Chabon's *The Amazing Adventures of The Escapist*.
He has won several Eisner Awards for his coloring work, and also colored
Tim Sale's art from the TV series *Heroes*.